Saint John

Rob Roy

NIMBUS
PUBLISHING LTD

95 96 97 98 99   5 4 3 2 1

Nimbus Publishing Limited
PO Box 9301, Station A
Halifax, NS B3K 5N5
(902) 455-4286

Design by Arthur B. Carter, Halifax
Printed & bound in Hong Kong

Canadian Cataloguing in Publication Data
Roy, Rob, 1953-
Saint John
ISBN 1-55109-117-8

1. Saint John (N.B.)—Pictorial works. I. Title.
FC2497.37.R69 1995   971.5'32 C95-950082-0
F1044.5.S14R69 1995

Title page: An intricately designed gargoyle watches over Prince William Street

Foreword

Side door of City Market
Oil painting (33″ x 21″) by Herzl Kashetsky

Saint John, New Brunswick—
Inspiration in a Major Port City

Saint John has inspired a wealth of images from artists, both past and present. The city has been depicted in paintings from the inside out: from its unique residents to its historical buildings, from the rise and fall of steep-hilled streets to the ebb and flow of the harbour tides.

From the high vantage point of Fort Howe hill in the city's north end, one can see in any direction and immediately grasp a panoramic view of Saint John. Together, the skyline and heritage give us a tangible sense of time that is apparent in architectural design and details.

There is not a street in Saint John that doesn't hold a potential photograph or painting to the perceptive eye. It might be a row of wooden utility poles extending like dominoes with a network of licorice wires that captures the eye, or perhaps a Victorian home, a stained glass window, a widow's walk, or a gargoyle's stony face gazing downward. Textures of warm, red brick or dark sandstone surround many arched entrances or carved wooden doors, inviting a closer look.

The colourful wooden houses and rooftops suggest interesting patterns of interlocking shapes. The observation deck of City Hall affords a fascinating perspective of uptown rooftops. In the heart of the city, the flutter of pigeon wings can create unusual rhythms and intricate patterns amidst King's Square.

Adjacent to the square is the City Market that has been a popular subject for many artists. One painting in particular comes to mind of a side door with all its chips and scratches conveying the movement of a generation of passersby.

Just as the weather alters the land, so is the city transformed: when fog enshrouds it in mystery, or when a winter snowfall leaves in its wake a series of clean, irregular surfaces. Warm sunlight casts cool shadows onto buildings—silhouettes beneath a pale sky.

A different time of day or year can bring a fresh experience to the same location. Although I began painting and drawing Saint John as a teenager, to this day when I retrace my footsteps, there is always something new to see or a new way to see something familiar. Inspiration and charm are waiting to be discovered and enjoyed. Whether your interest lies in culture or nature, you can delight in the experience of this oldest incorporated port city in Canada.

Herzl Kashetsky BFA, LLD
Artist

Blockhouse at Fort Howe

A re-creation on the site of a late 18th-century fort, the Blockhouse
stands as a lonesome sentinel overlooking the harbour.

Introduction

*The Cultural and Industrial Heritage
of Saint John, New Brunswick*

Saint John, New Brunswick, is a modest city. Nestled around the mouth of the Saint John River, it resolutely stands through the capricious weather off the Bay of Fundy. Hewn from the unforgiving rocky shore, the decisively geometric layout of Saint John's streets attests to the determination of its original settlers. This conviction makes Saint John proud of its past and keeps its traditions alive.

The written history of Saint John dates to 1604. Archaeological evidence of inhabitation however, has been dated to a period roughly four thousand years ago. A site on the edge of the harbour has shown signs of occupation by the Red Paint People, a group named for a characteristic red ochre or iron oxide earth they used for decorative purposes.

The Maliseet, the area's native people, have lived along the Saint John River for the past fifteen hundred years and would portage around the curiously reversing falls at the river's mouth and gather at the harbour during the summer months. It was this gathering place that is described by Samuel de Champlain in the first recorded instance of European exploration of the area in 1604. Champlain, the official cartographer from a French expedition led by Pierre de Gua de Monts, made a map of the area when his group entered the harbour and surveyed the mouth of the river on 24 June, the feast day of Saint John the Baptist. On the shore they encountered a Maliseet village, Ouigoudi, and traded with the chieftain, Chkoudoun. Thus began an association that would prove fortuitous for the French and lead the way in the European settlement of the region.

A little over a quarter of a century later the French established a more permanent presence in the area. By the end of 1632, a fortification was built on the shore of the harbour by Charles de St. Etienne de La Tour, an ambitious and powerful trader. One of the most poignant episodes in Saint John's history is the desperate struggle of La Tour's wife, Françoise Jacquelin, who attempted the defence of the fort during the absence of her husband. In the spring of 1645, Charles de Menou d'Aulnay, La Tour's rival, besieged the fort, captured it, and breaking his promise of clemency, executed all the prisoners while forcing Jacquelin to watch. She did not long survive the defeat; three weeks later she died while imprisoned.

The British era began more than a century later, in 1758, when the small French settlement at the mouth of the river was captured and dispersed by

Architecture on Prince William and King streets

Brunswick House and Old Mercantile Bank Building at the foot of King Street.

troops under the command of Colonel Robert Monckton. A new fortification, Fort Frederick, was built on the west side of the harbour and about three hundred soldiers were stationed there. In 1762, a group of New England traders and merchants established a trading post to take advantage of the vast resources of fur and timber that made their way down the river. Life in the settlement was not easy. The frequent attacks by marauding privateers from New England culminated in the destruction of Fort Frederick in 1775 while its defences were weakened—their troops had been called to fight the rebels in New England. Only after 1778, when Fort Howe was constructed on a strategically prominent hill overlooking the harbour, was there really effective defence of the settlement.

The end of the American Revolutionary War marked the most dramatic change for Saint John. In the spring of 1783, a fleet of ships arrived in the harbour from the American states carrying the first of fourteen thousand refugees loyal to the British Crown. However, inclement weather did not allow these Loyalists to disembark for a week. Today 18 May is celebrated as Loyalist Day in Saint John.

Originally there were two Loyalist settlements established at the mouth of the Saint John River, Parr Town, and on the opposite side of the harbour, Carleton. After New Brunswick was partitioned from Nova Scotia in 1784, a royal charter was granted by King George III and the two towns were combined to form Canada's first incorporated city, Saint John. Although it was considered the most likely location for the seat of the province's government, Saint John's heated political struggles resulted in the governor's decision to choose Fredericton, ninety-six kilometres up the Saint John River, as the provincial capital. Despite this early setback, the ideal location for the city resulted in its steady growth, both in population and industry, throughout the late eighteenth and early nineteenth centuries.

As New Brunswick's major port city, Saint John experienced both the promise and tribulation that accompany immigration. Great influxes of people have shaped the city's character in all periods of its development. In the late 1700s, Scottish and English immigrants were accommodated within a population that shared general similarities of language and religion. Not so easily absorbed into the fabric of the city were the great waves of destitute emigrants from Ireland, who needed assistance in their attempt to escape the desperation of the potato famines of the 1830s and 1840s. The stress placed upon the city erupted in one of its most ignominious incidents—the riots between Protestant and Catholic Irish on 12 July 1849, when violence claimed at least a dozen victims. Today, Saint John celebrates its cultural diversity in a week–long festival that encourages the understanding and appreciation of its ethnic mosaic.

Like most major cities in the 1800s, Saint John saw its share of destructive fires. The great conflagrations of 1837 and 1877 razed the central core of the city but relief efforts and civic pride spurred a great rebuilding. The results are sections of the city that have changed little in appearance for the last century, retaining some of the best examples of late nineteenth-century architecture in Atlantic Canada. The Victorian charm at the city's centre is accentuated by urban renewal efforts that began in the 1960s, amalgamation with neighbouring villages, and the development of burgeoning suburbs.

The prosperity brought about by Saint John's extensive involvement in shipping began to wane as the Age of Sail drew to a close. The city had always been New Brunswick's most industrialized area, and new approaches to attracting investment ensured that this role would continue. Saint John undertook to promote its location as one of only two ice–free winter ports in eastern Canada and also advocated its advantages as a tourist destination. An important terminus on contemporary transportation systems, the city continues to look forward to its role in international trade. Still the major port on the Bay of Fundy and the largest city in New Brunswick, Saint John maintains its position as one of the most significant urban influences on the social, economic, political and cultural life of the Maritimes.

Peter J. Larocque
Curator, History and Photography
New Brunswick Museum

Uptown and Harbour Bridge

Viewed across a span of the Harbour Bridge that links the uptown core and west Saint John, the city's modern skyline gives an accurate impression of its modest scale.

Preceding pages: Saint John from Fort Howe

The panoramic vista from this vantage point high above the city centre has been a favourite of artists and photographers for two centuries.

Lantic Sugar Refinery

Strategically located at the easternmost point of the harbour, the Lantic Sugar Refinery easily receives raw materials, which it processes into sweet products and then exports.

Princess of Acadia loading

Strong ties between Digby, Nova Scotia, and Saint John have existed since the late 18th century. That tradition continues with the automobile and passenger ferry service that is maintained today.

Loyalist House

An example of Georgian architecture at its finest, this home, which originally belonged to the Merritt family, is preserved in uptown Saint John as a monument to the fortitude and perseverance of New Brunswick's Loyalist families who founded the city in the late 18th century. Its hip roof, four chimneys, and transom light typify the order and balance of early 19th-century Saint John architecture.

Facing page: Delancey's Brigade

An 18th-century re-creation one could encounter in Canada's "Loyalist" city is Delancey's Brigade. In contemporary costume and supported by their families, the Brigade re-enacts parts of the American Revolution.

BARTON'S
TAKE OUT
SLOCUM & FERRIS
ESTABLISHED 1894
A DAY IN LIFE
Deli

Top left: City Market ceiling

Many Saint Johners believe that the ceiling timbers of the City Market have been inspired by construction techniques used in shipbuilding.

Top right: Germain Street entrance to the City Market

Recently, a newly remodelled and enhanced Germain Street entrance to the City Market was completed. Taking its inspiration from the architecture of the market building, the new addition also contains a subterranean tunnel that connects it to Brunswick Square.

Left: The City Market

Built in 1876, Saint John's City Market has been recognized as a national historic site. Canada's oldest covered market was fortunate to have escaped the fire of 20 June 1877 that laid waste a vast swath of the city's centre.

Facing page: City Market, interior

City Market comes alive during the day with sights and sounds from merchant stalls; some have been around for more than a century.

15

South Side of King Street

Looking much as they did a century ago, the red brick and olive
sandstone of the facades along the south side of King Street still
provide Saint John with its Victorian appeal.

King Street at night

Once the hustle and bustle of the business day is over, King Street, with its gleaming lights, takes on the qualities of a modern downtown and sheds its historical personality.

Facing page: Ice fishing on the Kennebecasis River

Every year during the smelt run, ice fishing shacks mushroom almost instantaneously on the January ice of the Kennebecasis River.

Exhibition Park Raceway

The quarter-mile oval of the Exhibition Park Raceway continues a longstanding tradition of horseracing in Saint John and is one of the few remaining racetracks in the Maritimes.

Left: Centenary Queen Square United Church

The scale and complexity of this soaring view perfectly illustrate the best in High Victorian Gothic architecture.

Below: Centenary Queen Square United Church, door hinge

The ornate iron hinges gracing the doors of Centenary Queen Square Church reflect the influence of Medieval architecture.

Facing page: Simeon Jones house or Caverhill Hall

Originally built for Simeon Jones, one of Saint John's renowned distillery owners, this house was constructed on the ruins of Jones' home that had been destroyed in the infamous fire of 20 June 1877.

Above: Ned Landry, international fiddling champion

Saint John, like the rest of the Maritimes, offers toe-tapping melodies of expert fiddlers. Few excel like Ned Landry and his accompaniment who give outstanding performances.

Right: Market Square, interior

Award-winning Market Square is the re-adaptation of late 19th-century commercial warehouses into a modern facility that includes a convention centre, hotel, retail shops, and the Saint John Regional Library. In addition, a newly renovated expansion features exhibitions and programmes of the New Brunswick Museum at this waterfront location.

Facing page: Horse and carriage at Market Square

Mark Hovey with his horse and carriage provide a more leisurely opportunity to survey the historic sights of Saint John.

Following pages: Germain Street

The projecting bay windows and contrasting sandstone details typify the red brick homes built along Germain Street in the late 19th century. This area continues to be a very fashionable locale for prosperous business people and professionals.

Loyalist Days Parade

Capping the events of the week-long Loyalist Days Festival in Saint John are the floats and bands of the Loyalist Days parade. For over two decades, historic re-creations and modern entertainment have celebrated Saint John's multicultural heritage during this popular festival.

Saint John has hosted the summertime entertainment event Buskers on the Boardwalk since 1990. Buskers, or street entertainers, ply their trade in uptown Saint John for a long weekend during the summer.

Above: Busking in uptown Saint John: "Glenn Singer"

Glenn Singer's physical comedy routines often involve audience participation. He has amused spectators around the world, including Europe and Asia.

Right: Busking in uptown Saint John: "Duo Anti-pasto"

Some buskers can never be too young, such as this local duo of classical musicians.

Courthouse spiral staircase

The engineering marvel of the self-supporting spiral staircase is still in daily use.

Facing page: Saint John County Courthouse

Designed by John Cunningham in 1840 and built in 1842, the Saint John County Courthouse has been the site of controversial trials and has had its own dramatic moments as well. Completely gutted by fire in 1919, the building was refurbished soon afterwards and still stands today on the eastern vista of King Square.

Parkerhouse Inn

Parkerhouse Inn on Sydney Street is renowned not only for the attention to detail that it gives its clients but also for the amount of detail evident in the delicately carved newels of its main staircase, the engraved intricacy of its door hinges, and the elegance of its decor.

Old City Hall

Built on the corner of Prince William and Princess streets, the site of a former City Hall, this building with its time-worn and blackened facade now houses small business enterprises.

Dredging the harbour

A common sight in the harbour is the dredging of the silt that has been deposited by the Saint John River. This is necessary to provide proper docking facilities for the continuous harbour traffic.

West side docks

Located in one of eastern Canada's two year-round ice-free harbours, the west side docks of the Port of Saint John are the terminus of transportation links that include the railway and trucking fleets.

33

Above: Moosehead Breweries

Tracing its development back to Susannah Oland's recipe for an English ale, the modern brewing company is managed by her descendants. The popularity of their products continues to grow internationally.

Crosby Molasses Company Limited

One of Saint John's prominent businesses, Crosby's was incorporated in 1906. The Crosby name is inseparable from the molasses that they sell across Canada and in New England. The firm's main processing and packaging plant on Rothesay Avenue has kept abreast of the latest marketing, research, and processing developments.

Facing page, inset: NB Tel

From its Saint John head office, the New Brunswick Telephone Company administers a state-of-the-art international telecommunications network.

House on Hazen Street

Typical of Italianate-inspired architecture are the tall windows, square, projecting tower, and assymetrically balanced structure of this brick and sandstone house on Hazen Street.

Buckingham Apartments, Orange Street

The curved steps of this building's stairs provide a welcoming prospect that highlights the majestic appearance of its towers, polished granite columns, and elaborately carved window accents.

Aquatic Driving Range

Saint John golfers can enjoy the unique facilities offered at Rockwood Park Golf Course's Aquatic Driving Range, the only one of its kind in the Maritimes.

Facing page: Fundy Cycling Club Race on Prince William Street

With its starting line on what was once Saint John's primary business street, the Cobblestone Classic is an annual event that raises the profile of cycling in the region.

Preceding pages: Panorama of the Reversing Falls

Spectators of the Reversing Falls Rapids have been mesmerized by this natural curiosity. There is a First Nations legend regarding its creation by Glooscap. The mouth of the Saint John River is spanned by the cantilever railway bridge and the spandrel arch bridge, which was built in 1914.

Carleton Martello Tower

From its vantage point high atop a promintory in West Saint John, Carleton Martello Tower has a spectacular view of the harbour and city. Begun in 1813 as a defensive measure during the War of 1812, the tower was not completed until 1815 when the war was over. In 1923 the tower was declared a national historic site and has been refurbished to indicate the most important moments of its past.

Carleton Martello Tower, interior

Carleton Martello Tower is currently maintained by Parks Canada as a museum that shows various aspects of its development. The powder magazine is restored to the 1840s period and the barrack floor is furnished to the period preceding Canada's Confederation in 1867. At one time, martello towers had a role in the defense of Canadian territory.

Above: Russian *Pliqué-à-jour* centrepiece bowl

The New Brunswick Museum houses collections relating to the natural and social history of New Brunswick. It also treasures its collection of international decorative arts from Asia, Europe, and Africa. This magnificent enamelled bowl is the work of Pavel Ovchinnikov of Moscow and was completed around the turn of the 20th century.

Left: Maliseet decorative art

The skill and artistry of New Brunswick's native peoples are represented in the collections of the New Brunswick Museum by items such as this deerskin and beadwork costume made in 1888 at the St. Mary's Reserve near Fredericton, New Brunswick, for Frank B. Hazen.

Facing page: The New Brunswick Museum

Designed by E. Claire Mott and built during the depths of the Great Depression, the columns and triangular pediment reflect the order and balance inspired by classical antiquity and are the most visible architectural features of the New Brunswick Museum on Douglas Avenue.

Irving Oil Refinery

Saint John is home to Canada's largest oil refinery. It is one of the
many successful industrial enterprises begun by New Brunswick's
entrepreneur K. C. Irving.

Saint John Shipbuilding Limited Dry Dock

Originally built in the early 1920s, the dry dock facilities, which are
used in the construction and repair of oil tankers, frigates, and cargo
vessels, carry on Saint John's shipbuilding traditions.

Facing page: Mercantile Centre

Mercantile Centre reflects the synthesis of old and new with stylized elements borrowed from adjacent historic properties combined with glass and steel characteristic of the late 20th century.

University of New Brunswick at Saint John campus

Since 1964, a branch campus of the University of New Brunswick has been located in Saint John. The present site of UNBSJ is located in Millidgeville, a suburb just outside the city centre, and boasts a commanding view of the Kennebecasis River.

Above: Plasterwork detail, Imperial Theatre

Gracefully adorning the cartouche above a doorway, these cherubs are the work of third-generation master craftsman Jean-François Furieri, who supervised the replacement and decoration of most of the intricate plasterwork in the theatre.

Left: Imperial Theatre

The newly refurbished and re-opened Imperial Theatre is one of the city's most impressive cultural structures. A group of devoted citizens inspired by memories of the past grandeur of the building combined with the assistance of federal, provincial, and municipal governments to realize a dream.

Imperial Theatre, interior

Providing one of the best facilities for the performing arts in Atlantic
Canada, the re-creation of the Imperial Theatre's original 1913 interior
is a pleasure to experience.

Residence on Princess Street

The striking presence of this house is due to the fully accented elements of its Second Empire style. The projecting central bay with tower, mansard roof, arched window, and door surrounds provide an arresting contrast with its central solid form.

House on Douglas Avenue

Typically Queen Anne in style, this home features a circular corner tower with a pointed turret, a variety of window forms, and an asymmetrically placed double-bayed porch to give a picturesque effect.

Swimming and sunbathing at
Rockwood Park's Fisher Lakes

Fun and relaxation are only a few minutes
away from the city centre in Rockwood
Park's 2,200 acres of natural environment.
The Fisher Lakes are a focal point with
sandy beaches for a refreshing swim.

Royal Kennebecasis Yacht Club

For a century the Royal Kennebecasis Yacht Club has provided mooring services to local and visiting yachters. Built in 1901, the clubhouse has been the scene of much hospitality and friendly competition.

Saint John String Quartet

The Church of St. Andrew and St. David is one of the many locations where musical enthusiasts can enjoy the performances of David Adams, Enoch Kwan, Christopher Buckley, and Sonja Adams whose talents have captivated audiences throughout Canada, the United States, and Japan.

Trinity Church

The design for Germain Street's Trinity Church was based upon William T. Thomas' drawing submitted to an advertised competition calling for a replacement of the original building that had been destroyed on 20 June 1877. The epitome of High Victorian Gothic architecture, Trinity Church features pointed arch windows, varied stonework textures, and a strongly emphasized sense of vertical lines.

Festival By the Sea: "Playdough Fish"

The brainchild of a group of Saint John High School students, Playdough Fish and their musical antics charmed audiences during the Children's Festival segment of Festival By the Sea.

Facing page: Festival By the Sea: Acadian dance troupe

One of the many popular multicultural aspects of Festival By the Sea is the Acadian Showcase that features the singers, dancers, and musicians of *La Marée Dansante*.

Cathedral of the Immaculate Conception, Waterloo Street

Begun in the 1850s to service Saint John's growing Irish population, the Cathedral of the Immaculate Conception features a profusion of buttresses and finials, as well as a circular stained-glass window over the entrance, that were inspired by the French Gothic style.

St. John's (Stone) Church

Built between 1824 and 1825, the Gothic Revival details of this
church make it one of the first such stone buildings in North America.
The intricately carved spires, which were the finishing touch, were
completed in 1826.

Old post office building,
Prince William Street

This stately example of the Second
Empire Style was built by the Canadian
government to replace a building that had
been destroyed in the Great Fire of 1877.
Conscious of safety features that would
make fire fighting easier, the building
features a flattened Mansard roof and was
Saint John's first completely iron-framed
structure.

Facing page: Aitken Bicentennial
Exhibition Centre

A modest example of Beaux-Arts
Classicism, the ABEC features the
characteristic columns and monumental
flight of steps associated with this style.
When it opened at the end of 1904,
people were delighted with such
architectural details as its highly
decorated, domed central rotunda.
Originally built as the Free Public Library
(with the assistance of Andrew Carnegie),
it now houses a variety of exhibition
spaces from art to interactive science
displays.

Since the mid-1980s, Saint John has hosted an outstanding festival that features the talents of performing artists from across Canada. Festival By the Sea creates a mood of excitement as residents and tourists enjoy live entertainment.

Festival By the Sea: "DancEast"

This group of young Canadian dancers, with their unique blend of classical, modern, and jazz choreography, first appeared at Festival By the Sea in 1993.

Sunset at Tucker Park

Lying at the confluence of the Kennebecasis and Saint John rivers, Indian and Goat islands are silhouetted against a vivid sunset when viewed from this popular swimming spot in the north end of the city.

Rhoda's Flea Market on King Street

A weekly event that is usually located indoors at Exhibition Park in the city's east end, Rhoda's Flea Market sometimes changes venue for those in search of news and bargains and takes on the character of an open air market.

Above: New Brunswick crafts

New Brunswick artisans are making award winning crafts that are internationally recognized for their creativity, workmanship, and design.

Right: Hand-painted clothing

The clothing produced under Susan and Maureen Hooper's "Sumo" label are brightly coloured and suggest a sense of quirky fun.

67

Left and facing page: Residential doorways

The type of reception anticipated when approaching a home can be determined by the doorway.

Following pages: Young Monument, King Square

Surrounded by the splendour of a flowerbed in full bloom, the 1891 Young Monument commemorates the efforts of a Saint John man's heroic but tragic attempt at rescuing a child who drowned in the frigid waters of Courtenay Bay.

69

Interior of house on Douglas Avenue

Inside, the doorways are enhanced with elaborate grillwork and the vista culminates in an oval stained-glass window manufactured at Gregory's own glassworks.

Facing page: House on Douglas Avenue

Built before World War I for a prominent lumber merchant, J. F. Gregory, this Queen Anne inspired house features a textural use of contrasting shingles, denticulation along the eaves, a semi-circular projecting tower, and a columned portico with balcony.

Right: Loyalist Burial Ground

Nestled in the heart of uptown Saint John, the final resting place of many of the city's first residents is a constant reminder of the hardships faced by the city's early settlers.

Below: Shaarei Zedek Cemetery

The chapel at Shaarei Zedek Cemetery keeps quiet vigil amidst the gravestones that commemorate members of Saint John's Jewish community.

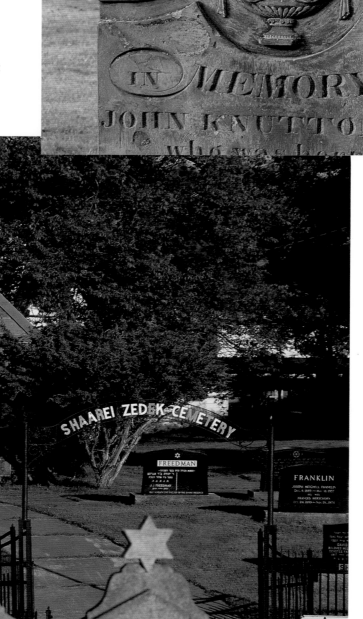

Assumption Church, West Saint John

Assumption Church on Dufferin Row, West
Saint John, was dedicated on 4 May 1907. Its
design is clearly derived from Byzantine and
Romanesque prototypes associated with early
Christianity.

Seaman's Mission on Prince William Street

Local woodworkers Mike and Roy Kippers provided the sign with carved rope and ship motifs that signals the entrance to the Seaman's Mission, a gathering place for seafarers when in port.

Thomas Furlong's Commercial Building

Built on the corner of Water and Princess streets, this building originally housed the store and warehouse of a wine and liquor merchant. A careful blending of many High Victorian architectural forms, one of the Gothic qualities of this structure is its naturalistic carved foliage and gargoyles.

Karen Shackleton and Herzl Kashetsky

Local artists like Karen Shackleton and Herzl Kashetsky contribute to the cultural heritage and fibre of the city.

NEW
POST
OFFICE
carved by
John Hooper
On this site
ext to Marsh
Creek, ships
were built by
woodworkers an
other craftsmen
of Saint John

John Hooper's sculpture

Located at the entrance to the Federal Post Office Building on Rothesay Avenue, John Hooper's grouping of life-sized sculptures captures a moment in time with elements of whimsical humour.

Wentworth Street looking north

A patchwork of roofs and windows, brick and board characterize the architectural variety of one of Saint John's steeply inclined south-end streets.

Preceding pages: Panorama of Market Square

John Hooper and Jack Massey's *Timepiece* chronicles the changes that have occurred in Saint John's uptown core. Here also are found Market Slip, Loyalist Plaza, North Market Wharf, St. Patrick Street, and City Hall graced by the modern sculpture of one of New Brunswick's Acadian artists, Claude Roussel.

Union Street looking west

Lining the length of the street, a queue of telephone poles mimics
a lane of traffic along one of Saint John's busiest thoroughfares.

Market Slip Wharf

Adjacent to the Hilton Hotel, Market Slip Wharf provides docking facilities for sailing craft. As well, the Canadian Coast Guard vessels routinely leave for the Bay of Fundy from this site.

Fishing in Saint John Habour

Although not as prevalent as it once was, fishing in Saint John Harbour continues by a few licensed fisherman even today.

Following pages: Atlantic National Exhibition

Beginning in 1818, Saint John has hosted fairs and exhibitions. Today the ANE, commonly referred to as "Th'Ex," is enjoyed for its carnival atmosphere as summer draws to a close.

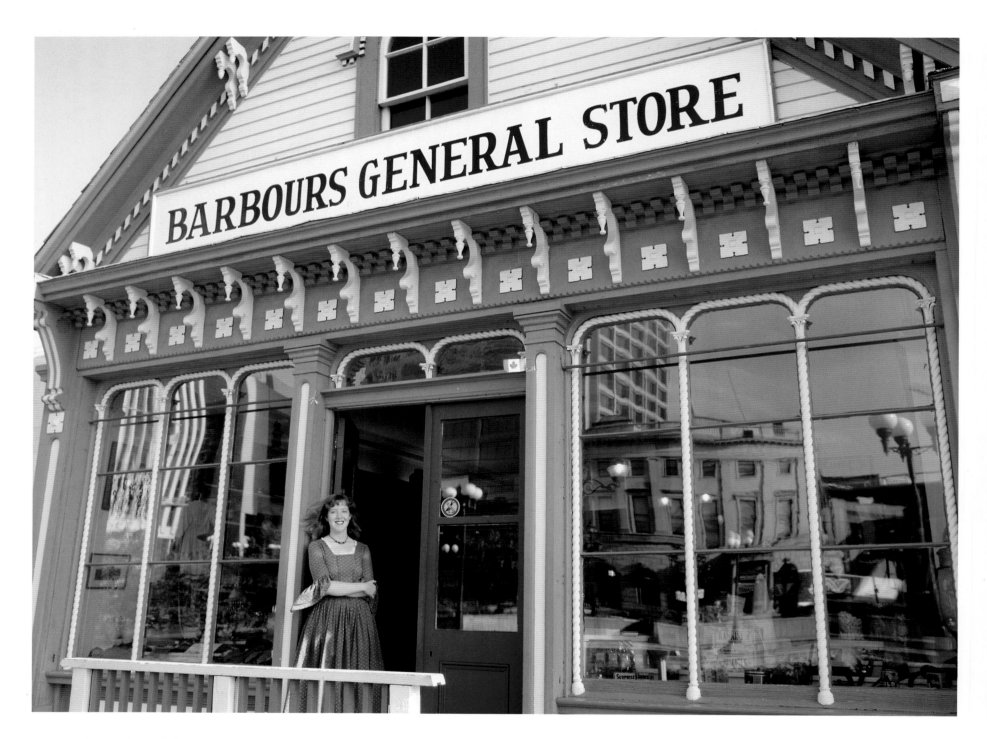

Barbours General Store

Relocated to the Market Square and refurbished as a centennial project
in 1967, Barbours General Store was originally from Sheffield in
Sunbury County. It is filled with examples of the practical foodstuffs
available to the mid-19th-century shopper.

House on Douglas Avenue

Based on the forms of the Italianate style, this Douglas Avenue house has a square-pillared porch and two tall towers. It deviates, however, in its unique use of varied window styles and placement.

House at Coburg and Garden streets

Irregularly massed and featuring a round turreted tower, the contrasting painted wood elements and decorative brickwork combine for a rather austere version of the Queen Anne style.

91

Gargoyles

While walking the length of Prince William Street, one sometimes has an uneasy sense of being observed. High above the street, the comings and goings of pedestrians and traffic are surveyed by a varied hoard of stoney-faced gargoyles, each with a unique story to tell.

Orange Street fence

Homeowners in the newly rebuilt streets of Saint John delineated their properties with the unmistakeable boundaries of intricate cast iron fences complete with sandstone posts.

Following pages: Harbour view with the cruise ship *Fascination*

Saint John's friendliness and facilities have made the port a popular destination for cruise ships from New England. Passing the massive cranes used for transferring containers to ships, the equally mammoth *Fascination* makes her way into the harbour.

Ruel Fountain at Fernhill Cemetery

The fountains and stately memorials that have been raised to Saint John citizens since 1848 entice one to contemplate the passage of time.